Franz Liszt

(1811–1886)

Albumblätter und kleine Klavierstücke

Album Leaves and Short Piano Pieces
Feuilles d'albums et pièces courtes pour piano

Nils Franke and Ateş Orga

ED 9054
ISMN 979-0-001-18696-4

Mainz • London • Berlin • Madrid • New York • Paris • Prague • Tokyo • Toronto
© 2012 SCHOTT MUSIC Ltd, London • Printed in Germany

Franz Liszt

(1811-86)

Albumblätter und kleine Klavierstücke
Album Leaves and Short Piano Pieces
Feuilles d'albums et pièces courtes pour piano

Auswahl und Kommentare von / Sélection et commentaires par / Selection and commentaries by

Nils Franke & Ateş Orga

ED 9054
ISMN 979-0-001-18696-4

Acknowledgements

The Editors wish to thank Dr Leslie Howard for generously making available his editions of Mariotte and Magyar.

Inhalt / Contents / Sommaire /

Seite/
Page

Die Stücke / The Pieces / Les pièces

4

Vorwort

„Das Klavier ist der Mikrokosmos der Musik"
~ Liszt, 18 Dezember 1877 ~

Kein anderer großer Pianist und Komponist der Romantik wird so mit dem Begriff der Klaviervirtuosität verbunden wie Franz Liszt (1811-86). Er war nicht nur ein hervorragender Pianist, sondern schuf auch einige der einflussreichsten Kompositionen des 19. Jahrhunderts, viele davon für das Klavier. Kein Wunder also, dass seine Fähigkeiten als Pianist sein künstlerisches Schaffen als Komponist prägten, was dazu führte, dass seine Klavierkompositionen eine große Herausforderung für die Pianisten und gelegentlich sogar für die Zuhörer darstellen. Trotzdem waren Liszts Werke, wie er selbst sagte, nicht auf Virtuosität ausgelegt; oftmals schien er sogar das Gegenteil zu bezwecken.

Die vorliegende Sammlung vereint Albumblätter und Fragmente, die Liszts Fähigkeit, einfach und doch ausgesprochen effektiv für sein Instrument zu schreiben, widerspiegeln. Bei der Auswahl der Stücke haben wir uns auf verschiedene Stilrichtungen in Liszts Werken von seinen Anfängen in jungen Jahren bis zu seinem Wirken als Abbé konzentriert. Dabei haben wir insbesondere einige seiner weniger bekannten Miniaturen berücksichtigt und den Schwerpunkt auf eine Zeit (von den 1840er- bis zu den 1860er-Jahren) gelegt, in der er die Wirkung seiner Klavierkompositionen bewusst weiterentwickelte – häufig durch Überarbeitungen extrem schwieriger früherer Werke.

Wir hoffen, dass Schüler und Lehrer durch unsere Auswahl zu einer intensiven Beschäftigung mit Liszts Musik angeregt werden, um die Zahl der Liszt-Anhänger, die seit Mitte des 20. Jahrhunderts stetig ansteigt, vielleicht noch etwas zu erhöhen.

Nils Franke & Ateş Orga
März 2011

Foreword

'The piano is the microcosm of music'
~ Liszt, 18 December 1877 ~

Of all the great Romantic pianist-composers, none is more intimately linked with the concept of keyboard virtuosity than Franz Liszt (1811-86). A performer of astonishing ability, Liszt produced some of the 19th century's most influential compositions, many conceived for his own instrument. Unsurprisingly, his skills as a pianist shaped his artistic output as a composer, resulting in an approach to piano scoring that makes heavy demands on players, occasionally even listeners. And yet much of Liszt's output was, by his own admission, not concerned with the projection of virtuoso skills; in many cases his intention appears to have been entirely the opposite.

The present collection draws together leaves and fragments reflecting Liszt's ability to write simply yet highly effectively for his instrument. In deciding our selection, we have focused on a breadth of styles within Liszt's output, from boyhood to venerated Abbé, in the process making a central case for some of his lesser-known miniatures, placing emphasis on a period (from the 1840s to the 1860s) during which he consciously refined the effectiveness of his own piano writing, often through clarifying revisions of transcendentally difficult earlier material.

We hope our choice will encourage students and teachers to explore Liszt's music in more detail, and that this in turn may contribute yet further to that community of Lisztians which has expanded so remarkably since the mid-20th century.

Nils Franke & Ateş Orga
March 2011

Préface

Parmi tous les grands compositeurs romantiques de musique pour le piano, aucun n'est lié plus intimement au concept de virtuosité pianistique que Franz Liszt (1811–1886). Lui-même interprète d'une extraordinaire virtuosité, Liszt composa des œuvres comptant parmi les plus marquantes du 19e siècle, dont une grande partie pour son propre instrument. Ainsi n'est-il pas surprenant que ses talents de pianiste aient influé sur son œuvre de compositeur, donnant lieu à des partitions très exigeantes pour les interprètes, voire parfois aussi pour les auditeurs. Et bien que de son propre aveu, la plus grande partie de son œuvre n'ait pas été écrite dans l'objectif de mettre la virtuosité en avant, ses intentions semblent avoir été complètement inverses dans de nombreux cas.

Le présent recueil réunit des pages et des fragments reflétant la capacité de Liszt à écrire à la fois simplement et efficacement pour son instrument. Pour notre sélection, nous avons puisé dans une large palette de styles représentatifs de son œuvre, de son enfance jusqu'à son état de vénérable abbé, tout en nous attachant particulièrement à certaines de ses miniatures moins connues, et à une période (des années 1840 à 1860) au cours de laquelle il travailla consciemment son style d'écriture, souvent par le biais de révisions destinées à clarifier des matériaux antérieurs extraordinairement difficiles.

Nous espérons que notre choix encouragera les élèves et leurs professeurs à explorer la musique de Liszt plus en détail et qu'en retour, cela apportera une contribution supplémentaire à la communauté de lisztiens qui s'est agrandie de manière si remarquable au cours de la seconde moitié du 20e siècle.

Nils Franke & Ateş Orga
Mars 2011

1. Walzer

S 208a

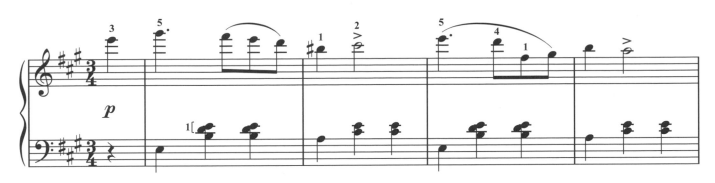

Fine

Da Capo al Fine

From Romantic Piano Anthology 2, ED 12913

2. Mariotte – Valse pour [?de] Marie

S 212a

3. Magyar

S 164e

4. Albumblatt Nr. 1

S 164

5. Feuilles d'Album

S 165

6. Albumblatt in Walzerform

S 166

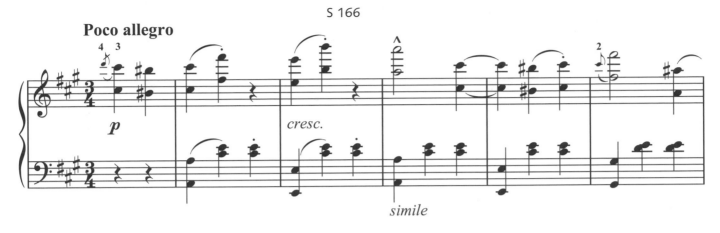

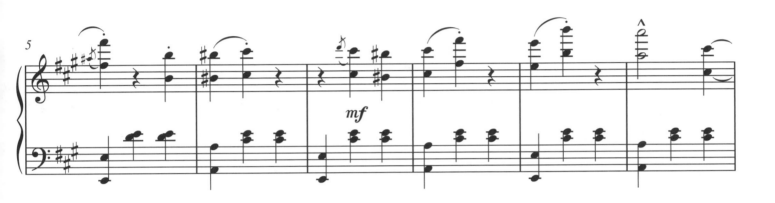

7. Ländler

S 211

8. Klavierstück No. 2

S 189a

From Romantic Piano Anthology 3, ED 12914

9. Notturno No. 2 [1ˢᵗ version]

S 541a [192a]

Lento espressivo

10. La cloche sonne

S 238

11. Klavierstück

S 193

12. Kleine Klavierstücke

S 192, No. 1

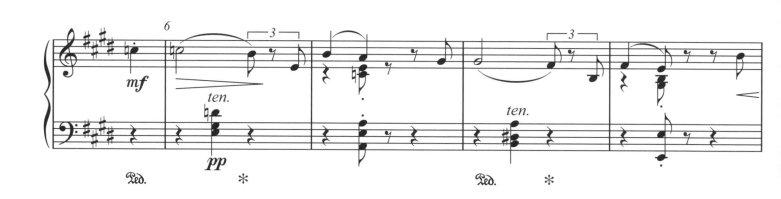

13. Kleine Klavierstücke

S 192, No. 2

14. Kleine Klavierstücke

S 192, No. 3

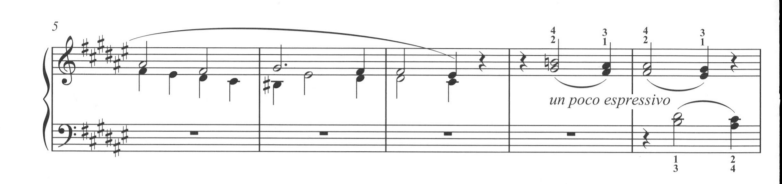

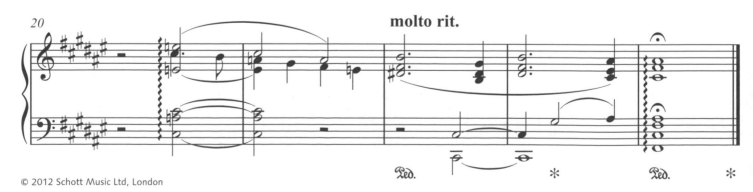

15. Kleine Klavierstücke

S 192, No. 4

From Romantic Piano Anthology 2, ED 12913

16. Kleine Klavierstücke, *Sospiri!*

S 192, No. 5

17. Geheimes Flüstern hier und dort

S 569, No. 10

18. Vergessene Romanze

S 527

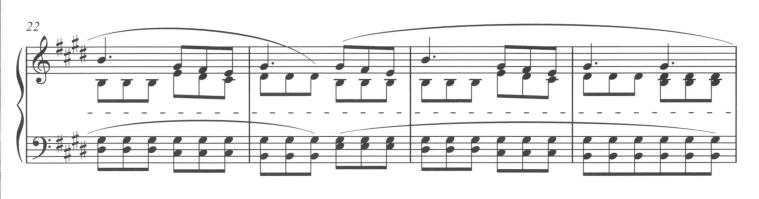

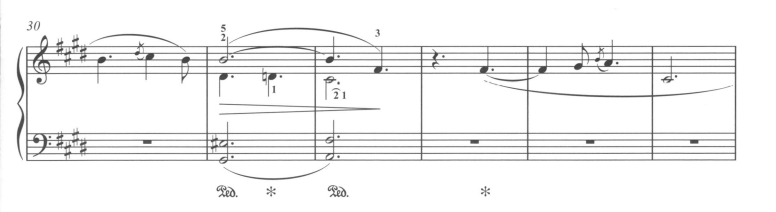

un poco rall.

Schott Music, London

Die Musik: Eine Einleitung

Liszts Werkkatalog enthält zahlreiche Fragmente und Miniaturen. Einige sind Skizzen für bekanntere Stücke, andere sind Neufassungen älterer Stücke. Nur wenige stellen eine technische Herausforderung dar. Auch wenn Liszt dafür bekannt ist, Emotionen auf dramatische Weise auszudrücken, so konnte er sie doch genauso gut durch zarte und zurückhaltende Klänge artikulieren. Die vorliegende Anthologie umfasst Liszts gesamtes Leben von 1823 bis 1880, von klassisch geprägten Stücken bis hin zu revolutionären Neuerungen. Dass er E, Fis, As und Des als besonders gefühlvolle Tonarten empfand und häufiger in Moll als in Dur komponierte, da es für ihn eher der Natur des einfachen Menschen entsprach, ist kein Zufall.

Walzer in A-Dur, S 208a, LW A2, Nr. 2 (?1823/25)
Ein Beispiel für „Master Listz" [sic], „gebürtiger Ungar", noch keine zwölf Jahre alt, in seiner offenkundigsten Schubert-Phase. Er schwelgt in Dominant- und Tonika-Akkorden (in dieser Reihenfolge) mit einem Mittelteil in E-Dur sowie in angenehm klaren Kontrasten zwischen *Legato*- und *Staccato*-Artikulation. Das Stück erschien in dem Wiener Ballett *Die Amazonen*, das 1823 von Graf Wenzel von Gallenberg (1783–1839), Ehemann der früheren Beethoven-Schülerin Giulietta Guicciardi, der die Mondscheinsonate gewidmet ist, „zusammengestückelt" wurde.

Mariotte–Valse pour [? de] Marie in As-Dur, S 212a, LW A82 (ca. 1840 [?1842])
Gräfin Marie d'Agoult (1805-76), Liszts Muse und Mutter seiner drei Kinder, begleitete ihn 1840 auf seine Reise nach Großbritannien und wohnte im Star & Garter Hotel in Richmond. Zu dieser Zeit war ihre Beziehung bereits zerbrochen. „Gestern [...] hast du kein einziges Wort gesagt, das nicht verletzend oder beleidigend sein sollte" (20. Juni). „Mein einziger, süßer, stärkender und grenzenloser Gedanke ist immer bei dir, meine entzückende und engelsgleiche Marie", schwärmte er (20. September). „[Dein] Genie und [unser/mein] Glück sind zwei unversöhnliche Feinde", konterte sie (22. September). Dieser Triolen-Walzer, der in ihrer Korrespondenz gefunden wurde, nimmt auf seltsame Weise die *dolce-/languido-* bzw. Dur-/Moll-Welt vorweg, die nach dem Bürgerkrieg durch Gottschalk in die amerikanische Salonmusik eingeführt wurde: die Verwendung des Vorschlags und der IIb-Akkorde spricht für sich.

Magyar in b-Moll/g-Moll, S 164e (1840)
Aus dem Londoner Gästebuch von Ignaz Moscheles (1794-1870), 3 Chester Place, Regent's Park. „2 juillet – 40". Liszt, so berichtete die Londoner *Times* an jenem Morgen, „ist jedem anderen Interpreten, ob auf dem Klavier oder einem anderen Instrument, meilenweit voraus." In den 28 Takten werden die wichtigsten Motive, Tonarten und Tempi der ersten Hälfte der *Magyar dalok* Nr. 11 skizziert, die 1843 in Wien erschien und zehn Jahre später die Grundlage für die dritte Ungarische Rhapsodie bildete. István Szelényi (1972) merkt an, dass „die von Liszt verwendeten Melodien [...] vermutlich aus den Teilen Ungarns stammen, in denen damals [1839-40] auch Rumänen lebten." Das Anfangsthema aus Tonika und Subdominante stammt aus einem traditionellen Soldatenlied: „Das Gras ist gefroren, friss es nicht, mein geliebtes Pferd/Bring mich heute Abend zu meiner Rose."

Albumblatt Nr. 1 in E-Dur, S 164, LW A66 (ca. 1840-41)
Diese Badinerie, eine Mischung aus *Moment musical*, *Consolation* und *Danse*, enthält Zitate aus dem *Valse mélancolique* (1839-40) und war zu Liszts Lebzeiten auf beiden Seiten des Atlantiks sehr bekannt. Der übermäßige Dreiklang, der zu Beginn über den Taktstrich hinweg gehalten wird und später wiederkehrt, erinnert daran, dass kein anderer Akkord aus Liszts harmonischem Repertoire so unauslöschlich *sein* musikalisches Markenzeichen war. (Die *Faust-Sinfonie* [1854-57] beginnt mit vier übermäßigen Dreiklängen in der Melodie, *Funérailles* [1849] endet auf einem übermäßigen Dreiklang, und der Höhepunkt von *Unstern!* [nach 1880] wird durch eine Verkettung von übermäßigen Dreiklängen intensiviert).

Feuilles d'Album in As-Dur, S 165, LW A104 (1841 [? 1844])
Dieses Stück, 1844 bei Schott erschienen, ist ein Konzertwalzer à la Chopin, in dem sich darüber hinaus im oktavierten (zweiten) Thema ein Schumannscher Papillon verbirgt.

Albumblatt in Walzerform in A-Dur, S 166, LW A83 (1842)
Ein modulierendes *soufflé* in verschiedenen Tonarten, am 5. Juni 1842 in Hamburg auf Liszts Rückreise von Russland nach Paris notiert.

Ländler in A-Dur, S 211, LW A95 (1843)
Die stereotypen österreichischen *Ländler* und *Walzer* in Liszts Werkkatalog weisen darauf hin, dass er während seiner Habsburger Jugend den Wiener Tänzen näher stand als den Tänzen aus Paris. In diesem schlichten *Allegretto* aus seinen Tourneejahren verbindet Liszt seine Affinität zu Dominant-/Tonika-Akkordfolgen (vgl. Walzer, S 208a) mit einem Anflug von Reue. Der Liszt der verhängnisvollen und zerbrochenen Affären.

Klavierstück Nr. 2 in As-Dur, S 189a, LW A116 (1844 [? 1845])
Das tänzerische *Feuille d'album* entstand während eines Spanien-Aufenthalts und zeichnet sich durch Geschmeidigkeit in Melodie und Tempo aus. Vier Jahre später übertrug Liszt das Hauptthema auf den Anfang und Schluss der Ersten Ballade. Chromatische Verzierungen und ein Anflug von *minore* am Ende verleihen dem Stück Spannung.

Notturno Nr. 2 in E-Dur, 1. Version, S 541a [192a] (ca. 1850 oder später)
Eine vereinfachte 21-taktige Skizze des *Liebestraums Nr. 2*, die 1850 veröffentlicht wurde [vgl. Klavierstücke, S 192/1]. Sie ist eine Bearbeitung eines Liedes von Liszt: *Seliger Tod (Gestorben war ich)*, nach einem Gedicht von

Johann Ludwig Uhland (1787-1862). „Gestorben war ich vor Liebeswonne; begraben lag ich in ihren Armen; erwecket ward ich von ihren Küssen; den Himmel sah ich in ihren Augen."

La cloche sonne, S 238, LW A169
(Die läutende Glocke, ca. 1850)
Dieses französische Volkslied in c-Moll wurde 1958 von Jack Werner veröffentlicht. Die von ihm hinzugefügte Jahreszahl 1850 (in Anlehnung an frühere Quellen) überzeugt Leslie Howard (1994) nicht. Er ist der Auffassung, dass die Musik „stärker an den späteren Liszt erinnert als an dessen frühen Jahre in Weimar." Dies ist zwar zutreffend, doch sollte berücksichtigt werden, dass in der Zeit nach Liszts Konzertjahren nicht nur der *Scherzo* und *Marsch* sowie die *Sonate in h-Moll* entstanden (1851-53), sondern auch das introvertierte, völlig andere Szenario der *Consolations* (1849-50) sowie einige der *Harmonies poétiques et religieuses* (1847-52).

Klavierstück in Fis-Dur, S 193 (nach 1860)
Über die Entstehung dieses Albumblattes, das 1928 von Liszts Schüler José Vianna da Motta herausgegeben wurde, ist nichts bekannt. Es wird vermutet, dass das vielschichtige Stück aus der „römischen"/Abbé-Phase des Komponisten stammt. Howard (1991) ist der Auffassung, das Stück sei „mit seinem ausgeprägten melodischen Bogen und seinen parallelen Terzen wesentlich stärker Liszts früherem Stil verhaftet", räumt jedoch „gar manchen Verweis" auf Liszts spätere, progressive Werke ein. Hier sollte die Polarität der Tonart Fis-Dur – Liszts „Segens-" und Scrjabins „blaue" Tonart – beachtet werden.

Kleine Klavierstücke, S 192, LW A233 (1865-79)
Diese fünf Miniaturen wurden für die Baronin Olga von Meyendorff (1838-1926) komponiert. 1871 verwitwet (ihr Mann war russischer Diplomat in Weimar gewesen), korrespondierte sie mit Liszt bis zu dessen Lebensende, eine Beziehung, die Fürstin Carolyne zu Sayn-Wittgenstein (1819-87) – Liszts „Ehefrau", die sie nie war – als „weit weniger unschuldig als eine bloße *amitié amoureuse*" (Adrian Williams, 1990) ansah. Die Miniaturen waren als unabhängige Stücke konzipiert und umfassen die so genannte „römische" und „vie-trifurquée"-Phase. Nr. 1 (E-Dur, Januar 1865) ist eine weitere Anlehnung an den *Liebestraum Nr. 2* [vgl. Notturno Nr. 2, S 541a], allerdings fünfzehn Jahre später. In dem dynamisch ähnlichen Stück Nr. 2 (As-Dur, Februar 1865) werden Akkorde auf unbetonten Zählzeiten in der Mittelstimme mit einem leidenschaftlichen Höhepunkt kombiniert. Nr. 3 (22. Juli 1873) und 4 (23. Juli 1876) sind Sonette in Fis-Dur, in denen sparsame und fein abgestimmte Klangintensivierungen im Vordergrund stehen. „Die echte Grundlage von [Liszts] Charakter ist Barmherzigkeit. *Das zerstoßene Rohr wird er nicht zerbrechen, noch das geängstigte und zerschlagene Herz verachten!*" (Amy Fay, 15. Juli 1873). Nr. 5, *Sospiri! (Seufzer!*, 23. Juli 1879), wurde 1969 veröffentlicht und kommt den späten Klavieraphorismen am nächsten. Das Stück steht zwar in As-Dur, beginnt und endet jedoch etwas rätselhaft, da der Grundton in einem Vakuum aus nicht aufgelösten verminderten Akkorden

untergeht. In den ersten zehn Takten kommen alle zwölf Töne der chromatischen Tonleiter vor. „Das Erstaunliche [einer solchen Musik] ist, dass sich Liszt der Atonalität schon [annäherte], bevor Schönberg etwa fünfundzwanzig Jahre später ‚die Luft von anderem Planeten' fühlte" (Alan Walker, 1970).

Geheimes Flüstern hier und dort, S 569, LW A264b, No. 10
(1874)
Diese Bearbeitung der dritten von Clara Schumanns sechs Hermann-Rollett-Vertonungen op. 23 (10. Juni 1853) stammt aus Liszts *Zehn Lieder von Robert und Clara Schumann*. Des-Dur: Leises Murmeln und Wälder. Liebe und Natur werden hier durch das Medium Lied vermittelt. In den 1850er-Jahren distanzierte sich Clara (1819-96), die unübertroffene Klaviervirtuosin unter den deutschen Romantikern, von Liszt so weit, dass sie sogar seine Widmung in beiden Versionen der *Grandes études de Paganini* (1838, 1851) ablehnte. Einst hatte sie ihn jedoch grenzenlos bewundert und die Begeisterung ihres Vaters geteilt: „Liszt […] kann man mit keinem anderen Pianisten vergleichen – er ist absolut einzigartig. Er erzeugt Angst und Erstaunen […] ein Original – völlig besessen vom Klavier […] Er hat eine großartige Seele; man kann über ihn sagen: ‚Seine Kunst ist sein Leben'"(Friedrich Wieck, *Tagebuch*, Wien, 12. April 1838). „Seit ich Liszts Virtuosität gehört und gesehen habe, fühle ich mich wie ein Schulmädchen" (Brief an Robert, 28. April 1838).

Vergessene Romanze in e-Moll, S 527, LW A299 (1880)
Während seines Aufenthalts in der Villa d'Este im Herbst 1880 komponierte Liszt eine *Romance oubliée* (*Vergessene Romanze*) für Viola und Klavier, S 132, die dem deutschen Virtuosen Hermann Ritter (1849-1926) gewidmet war. Gleichzeitig arbeitete er an Versionen für Violine, Cello und Soloklavier, die im darauffolgenden Jahr in Hannover gedruckt wurden. Der Ursprung dieses Stückes, dessen Textur eher an Liszts Spätwerk erinnert, dessen Ausdruckskraft jedoch aus seinen frühen Stücken stammen könnte, liegt in einer Romance oubliée für Klavier, S 169 (8. Juli 1848, „pour Madame Joséphine Koscielska"). Diese ging wiederum aus dem Lied *Oh pourquoi donc*, S 301a (1843) mit einem Text der russischen Dichterin und Schriftstellerin Karolina Pawlowa (1807-93) hervor. Die erste Hälfte im 9/8-Takt mit einer Kadenz auf der Mediante wird durch einen zweiten Teil im 6/8-Takt ausgeglichen, der zu E-Dur moduliert.

Ateş Orga

The Music: An Introduction

Fragments and miniatures crowd Liszt's catalogue. Some are sketches for more famous pieces. Others are latterday re-slantings. Few are pianistically daunting. Liszt may have been famous for thundering and gilding his emotions. But he could as readily convey feeling through reserved resonances and modest declamation. This anthology ranges across his life, from 1823 to 1880, from classically-schooled skills to prophetic newness. That he felt E, F sharp, A flat and D flat to be lyrically conducive keys, that the man in the field spoke to him more often in minor than major, is no coincidence.

Walzer in A major, S 208a, LW A2, No.2 (? 1823/25)
An example of 'Master Liszt' [sic], 'native of Hungary', not yet twelve, at his most obviously Schubertian, celebrating dominant and tonic harmonies (in that order), with a middle section in E major, and pleasingly unfussed contrasts of slurred and staccato articulation. The piece featured in a Viennese ballet, *Die Amazonen*, 'cobbled together' in 1823 by Count Wenzel von Gallenberg (1783–1839), husband of Beethoven's former student Giulietta Guicciardi, dedicatee of the *Moonlight* Sonata.

Mariotte – Valse pour [? de] Marie in A flat major, S 212a, LW A82 (c 1840 [? 1842])
Marie, Comtesse d'Agoult (1805-76), Liszt's muse and mother of his three children, joined him for part of his 1840 visit to Britain, staying at the Star and Garter Hotel, Richmond. By then, however, their relationship was fractured. 'Yesterday [...] you spoke not a single word which was not calculated either to hurt or offend' (20 June).'My sole, sweet, fortifying and unbounded thought is always with you, my delightful and angelic Marie', he would revere (20 September). '[Your] Genius and [our/my] Happiness are two irreconcilable enemies,' she would riposte (22 September). This *Valse* in triplets, secreted away in their correspondence, oddly anticipates the kind of *dolce/languido*, major/minor world that post-Civil War American parlour music, via Gottschalk, was to so atmospherically make its own: the use of appoggiatura and IIb harmony is telling.

Magyar in B flat minor/G minor, S 164e (1840)
From the London guestbook of Ignaz Moscheles (1794-1870), 3 Chester Place, Regent's Park. '2 juillet – 40'. Liszt, the London *Times* reported that morning, 'leaves every other performer, whether on the pianoforte or any other instrument, at an immeasurable distance behind him'. The 28 bars sketch the principal ideas, keys and tempi found in the first half of the Eleventh *Magyar dalok* published in Vienna in 1843, basis ten years later of the Third Hungarian Rhapsody. István Szelényi (1972) notes that 'the melodies Liszt uses [...] presumably come from those parts of Hungary that were then [1839-40] also inhabited by Rumanians'. The opening tonic/subdominant theme is from a traditional recruiting song: 'The grass is frosty, don't eat it my beloved horse/Take me to my rose tonight'.

Albumblatt No. 1, in E major, S 164, LW A66 (c 1840-41)
Crossing *moment musical*, *consolation* and *danse*, this trifle, quoting from the *Valse mélancolique* (1839-40), enjoyed favour during Liszt's lifetime, circulating on both sides of the Atlantic. The opening, and subsequently recurring, augmented triad, suspended across the barline, reminds that no other chord in Liszt's harmonic arsenal was so indelibly *his* soundprint. (Four linearisations launch the *Faust* Symphony [1854-57]; *Funérailles* [1849] expires to one; chain upon chain intensify the climax of *Unstern!* [post 1880].)

Feuilles d'Album in A flat major, S 165, LW A104 (1841 [? 1844])
Published in 1844 by Schott, this is in the style of a concert waltz *alla* Chopin, a ghostly Schumannesque *papillon* shadowing the octaved (second) subject.

Albumblatt in Walzerform in A major, S 166, LW A83 (1842)
A modulating, mode-shifting *soufflé*, jotted down in Hamburg, 5 June 1842, on Liszt's way back from Russia to Paris.

Ländler in A flat major, S 211, LW A95 (1843)
The presence of stereotypically Austrian *Ländler* and *Walzer* in the Liszt catalogue is affirmation that in his Habsburg youth he was closer to Viennese dance than Parisian. This delicately understated *allegretto* from the travelling years combines a fondness for dominant/tonic progressions (*cf* Walzer, S 208a) with touches of regret. The Liszt of fatal attractions and broken love affairs.

Klavierstück No. 2, in A flat major, S 189a, LW A116 (1844 [? 1845])
A terpsichorean *feuille d'album*, pliant in melody and tempo, sketched during a visit to Spain. Four years later Liszt lifted the principal idea, transposed down a fifth, for the outer sections of the First Ballade. Decorative chromaticism, and a touch of *minore* at the end, tension the canvas.

Notturno No. 2, in E major, 1st version, S 541a [192a] (c 1850 or earlier)
A simplified 21-bar sketch of the Second *Liebesträume* published in 1850 [cf Klavierstücke, S 192/1], transcribing one of Liszt's songs, *Seliger Tod* (*Gestorben war ich*), to lines by Johann Ludwig Uhland (1787-1862). 'I was dead from love's bliss; I lay buried in her arms; I was wakened by her kisses; I saw heaven in her eyes'.

La cloche sonne, S 238, LW A169 (*The tolling bell*, ? c 1850)
This French folksong setting in C minor was edited by Jack Werner in 1958. His appended 1850 dating (following earlier authorities) doesn't convince Leslie Howard (1994), who suggests that stylistically the music 'seems more redolent of the later Liszt world than it does of his early years in Weimar'. True – though worth remembering that the post-touring period which produced the Scherzo & March and B minor Sonata (1851-53) also witnessed

the introverted, very different scenario of the *Consolations* (by 1849-50) and several of the *Harmonies poétiques et religieuses* (1848-53).

Klavierstück in F sharp major, S 193 (post-1860)
Nothing is known about the provenance of this *Albumblatt*, edited in 1928 by Liszt's student José Vianna da Motta. Presumed to date from the composer's 'Roman'/Abbé phase, its language is eclectic. Howard (1991) senses an 'earlier style, with its fulsome melodic arch and parallel thirds', while yet acknowledging 'many a hint' of latter-day progressiveness. Its F sharp polarity – Liszt's 'benediction' key, Scriabin's 'blue' mode – should be noted.

Kleine Klavierstücke, S 192, LW A233 (1865-79)
These five miniatures were written for Baroness Olga von Meyendorff (1838-1926). Widowed in 1871 (her husband had been Russian envoy to Weimar), she corresponded with Liszt to the end of his life, a relationship Princess Carolyne Sayn-Wittgenstein (1819-87) - Liszt's 'wife' who never was - viewed as 'far less innocent than a mere amitié amoureuse' (Adrian Williams, 1990). Intended as independent pieces, they span Liszt's so-called 'Roman' and 'Vie Trifurquée' periods. No. 1 (E major, January 1865) takes another look at the Second *Liebesträume* [cf Notturno No 2, S 541a], fifteen years on. Related dynamically, No. 2 (A flat major, February 1865) combines offbeat middle-voice harmonies with an impassioned climax. Nos. 3 (22 July 1873) and 4 (23 July 1876) are rarefied F sharp major sonnets stressing economy and finely tuned intensifications of sound. 'The real *basis* of [Liszt's] nature is compassion. *The bruised reed he does not break, nor the humble and docile heart despise!*' (Amy Fay, 15 July 1873). Closest to the late keyboard aphorisms, No. 5, *Sospiri!* (*Sighs!*, 23 July 1879), published in 1969, orbits A flat major but opens and closes enigmatically, the keynote amberised in a vacuum of unresolved diminished harmonies. The first ten bars concentrate all twelve tones of the chromatic scale. 'The astonishing fact [in such music] is that Liszt [approached] atonality some twenty-five years before Schoenberg felt "the air of another planet"' (Alan Walker, 1970).

Geheimes Flüstern hier und dort, S 569, LW A264b, No.10
(*Secret Whispers*, 1874)
From Liszt's *Zehn Lieder von Robert und Clara Schumann*, this is an arrangement of the third of Clara's six Hermann Rollett settings, Op. 23 (10 June 1853). D flat major. Quiet murmurs and woodland spaces. Love and nature borne through song. By the 1850s Clara (1819-96), keyboard queen of the Teuton Romantics, had distanced herself from Liszt, to the point of rejecting his dedication of both versions of the *Grandes études de Paganini* (1838, 1851). Once though she had admired him unreservedly, sharing her father's enthusiasm: 'Liszt [...] cannot be compared with any other player – he is absolutely unique. He arouses fear and astonishment [...] an original – totally involved with the piano [...] He has a great soul; one may say of him, "His art is his life"' (Friedrich Wieck, *Diary*, Vienna

12 April 1838). 'Since hearing and seeing Liszt's *bravura* I feel like a schoolgirl' (letter to Robert, 28 April 1838).

Vergessene Romanze in E minor, S 527, LW A299 (1880)
While staying at the Villa d'Este during the autumn of 1880, Liszt composed a *Romance oubliée* for viola (viola alta) and piano, S 132, dedicated to the German virtuoso Hermann Ritter (1849-1926). Concurrently he also prepared versions for violin, cello and solo piano, printed in Hannover the following year. Pianistically *late* in texture but stylistically *early* in expressive resource, the origins of the piece lie in a *Romance oubliée* for piano, S 169 (8 July 1848, 'pour Madame Joséphine Koscielska'), derived from the song *Oh pourquoi donc*, S 301a (1843), to words by the Russian poet and novelist Karolina Pavlova (1807-93). The 9/8 first half, cadencing on the mediant, is balanced by a second section in 6/8, modulating to E major.

Ateş Orga

Anmerkungen für Lehrer und Schüler

Walzer in A-Dur, S 208a, LW A2, Nr. 2
Das früheste Stück dieser Sammlung lebt vom Kontrast zwischen *legato* und *staccato* gespielten Melodietönen.

Mariotte – Valse pour [? de] Marie in As-Dur, S 212a, LW A82
Dieser Walzer ist weder virtuos noch besinnlich, religiös oder dramatisch, sondern scheint weit von allem entfernt zu sein, was man mit Liszt verbindet. Stattdessen belegt er Liszts Fähigkeit zu bezaubern, fröhlich und unbeschwert zu sein. Er wurde in einem Brief des Komponisten an Marie d'Agoult gefunden und ist ein kurzes, jedoch sehr ausgewogenes Charakterstück. Die Melodie besteht jeweils aus dem ersten Ton der Triolengruppen, der vom Komponisten ab Takt 17 hervorgehoben wird. Um möglichst bald ein flüssiges Spieltempo zu erreichen, sollten die Triolengruppen jeweils als Viertelakkord geübt werden, bevor sie wie notiert gespielt werden.

Magyar in b-Moll/g-Moll, S 164e
Eine Wiederverwendung oder Überarbeitung von Themen oder sogar ganzen Werken, manchmal über einen Zeitraum von vielen Jahren, war Liszt nicht fremd. Obwohl dieses Albumblatt, das auf drei bekannten Melodien aus Liszts späteren Werken basiert, nicht zur Veröffentlichung bestimmt war, ist es eine hervorragende „Ungarische Rhapsodie in Miniaturform". Die wohl anspruchsvollste Passage befindet sich im *Piu animato*, nicht zuletzt wegen der erforderlichen Fingerspreizung in der linken Hand. Damit das Stück im Ganzen wirken kann, sollte das *Rallentando* am Schluss sowohl in Bezug auf die Dynamik als auch auf das Timing ein klarer Zielpunkt sein.

Albumblatt Nr. 1 in E-Dur, S 164, LW A66
Der Beginn dieses Stückes wird manchmal als unerwartet empfunden. Der übermäßige Akkord, der auf der Zwei des nachfolgenden Taktes aufgelöst wird, muss nicht über den Taktstrich hinweg gehalten werden. Man kann sich das His als allmähliches *Crescendo* vorstellen, fast wie einen Holzbläserton, um eine bessere Verbindung zum nachfolgenden Cis herzustellen.

Feuilles d'Album in As-Dur, S 165, LW A104
Dies ist eine spritzige Zugabe, eine Lisztsche Version des damals so populären Walzers. Der angegebene Fingersatz ist zwar zunächst vielleicht nicht besonders angenehm, doch lässt die Melodie ab Takt 13 nicht viel Raum für alternative Fingersätze. Man muss diese Passagen für jeden einzelnen Finger üben, damit sie flüssig gespielt werden können. Die vorgeschlagene Aufteilung der Passagen auf beide Hände wurde nachträglich hinzugefügt, ist jedoch sehr praktisch. Sie folgt dem Ansatz, dass letztendlich der Klang selbst zählt und nicht die Art und Weise, wie er erzeugt wird.

Albumblatt in Walzerform in A-Dur, S 166, LW A83
Das Stück ist zwar unkompliziert, jedoch gut geeignet, um Oktaven in der rechten und Sprünge in der linken Hand miteinander zu kombinieren. Solange die schwächeren Zählzeiten in der linken Hand der Melodie untergeordnet werden, spielt sich das Stück quasi von selbst. In Takt 14/15 sollte man bei der etwas unerwarteten Modulation nach Cis-Dur aufpassen.

Ländler in As-Dur, S 211, LW A95
In den ersten acht Takten bettet Liszt die Melodie in einen kontinuierlichen Achtellauf ein. Um ein besseres Hörverständnis für die Beziehung zwischen Bass- und Oberstimme zu entwickeln, sollte man diese Takte üben, indem man alle Töne in der rechten Hand weglässt, die nicht zur Melodie gehören.

Klavierstück Nr. 2 in As-Dur, S 189a, LW A116
Die größte Herausforderung der ersten acht Takte ist eine effektive Trennung von Melodie und Begleitung in der rechten Hand. Die unterstützenden Achtelfiguren in diesen Takten kehren in Takt 9 und 10 als Doppeltöne wieder – ein Aufbau, der an einige Begleitpassagen aus einem von Liszts erfolgreichsten lyrischen Konzertstücken, *Bénédiction de dieu dans la solitude*, erinnert. Die Wirkung des Stückes liegt hauptsächlich im exakten Spiel der Melodie, die gemäß der Spielpraxis im 19. Jahrhundert nicht immer mit den Basstönen auf der Eins im Takt zusammenfällt. Wenn man sich für eine (kleine) Verzögerung des ersten Melodietons im Takt entscheidet, anstatt ihn mit seinem dazugehörigen Ton in der linken Hand zu spielen, sollte man diesen Effekt sparsam und nur an zentralen Melodiestellen verwenden.

Notturno Nr. 2, in E-Dur, 1. Version, S 541a [192a]
Diese 21-taktige Miniatur hat einen sehr ausgewogenen ABA-Aufbau. Nur der Mittelteil (Takt 9-12) weicht von dem ansonsten oberstimmenorientierten Klanggefüge ab: Hier müssen sowohl Sopran- als auch Tenorstimme deutlich zu hören sein. Der Fingersatz für die rechte Hand in Takt 9 stammt von Liszt und bewirkt, dass die ersten vier Achtel ohne Lagenwechsel gespielt werden können. Anschließend neigt sich die Hand nach rechts und nimmt die nächste Position ein.

La cloche sonne, S 238, LW A169
Dieses Stück gehört zu Liszts technisch zugänglichsten Werken. Länge und Charakter deuten auf ein Albumblatt hin. Die größte Herausforderung des Werks ist, Melodie und Begleitung im Gleichgewicht zu halten, da die Melodie am Anfang und Schluss mit der linken und in Takt 13-25 mit der rechten Hand gespielt wird. Da der Weimarer Autograph keine Aufführungshinweise enthält, wurden die dynamischen Zeichen und Artikulationszeichen nachträglich hinzugefügt und sind somit nicht verbindlich.

Klavierstück in Fis-Dur, S 193
Dieses Stück weist sowohl Merkmale der jüngeren Vergangenheit als auch der nahen Zukunft seiner Zeit auf. In Bezug auf Tonart, wogende Bewegungen in der linken Hand und die Verwendung von Terzen in der Melodiestimme erinnert es ein wenig an Chopins Barcarolle op. 60 und antizipiert gleichzeitig die französische und russische Musik der Spätromantik. Der dynamische Höhepunkt des Stückes

wird durch die Scheinkadenz in Takt 22-24 erzeugt. Die musikalische Rastlosigkeit entsteht hauptsächlich durch die Spannung zwischen einem chromatisch fallenden Akkord und der rhythmischen Aufeinanderfolge zweier Achtel in einer Figur aus drei Achteln. Die Terzen ab Takt 30 lassen sich am besten als Folge aus Viertelakkorden erlernen, die aus den Noten der jeweiligen Terz bestehen.

Kleine Klavierstücke, S 192, LW A233

Diese fünf Werke, die über einen Zeitraum von vierzehn Jahren als unabhängige Miniaturen entstanden, belegen den Stilwandel des Komponisten von der starken Gefühlsbetontheit seiner Hauptwerke zu einem zunehmend introspektiven und harmonisch experimentellen Gefüge. Die stilistisch unkomplizierten beiden ersten Stücke enthalten noch typische Liszt-Merkmale: Am Schluss von Nr. 2 (ab Takt 43) ist die linke Hand so gesetzt, dass der fünfte Finger auf den ersten folgt (Takt 44), eine Technik, die Liszt mit großer Wirkung in den Tonleiterpassagen seiner *Rhapsodie espagnole* einsetzte, wenn auch in der rechten Hand (also Finger 5 zu 1). Nr. 3 und 4 sind etwas weniger dicht komponiert und weisen eine ruhigere Atmosphäre auf. Das fünfte Stück, *Sospiri*, ist wohl das innovativste von allen. Zwar bieten die arpeggierten Figuren in der linken Hand in Takt 38-57 noch eine harmonische Auflösung, der Schluss jedoch nicht mehr – das daraus resultierende musikalische Fragezeichen ist somit ein direkter Ausdruck der zukünftigen Unsicherheit, der die tonale Musik ausgesetzt war – zumindest sieht es rückblickend so aus. Die arpeggierten Figuren lassen zwei verschiedene Fingersätze zu, wie in den Noten angegeben. Es kann von Vorteil sein, beide zu lernen, nicht zuletzt deshalb, weil sich der Klang dieser Passage je nach Fingersatz erheblich ändern kann.

Geheimes Flüstern hier und dort, S 569, LW A264b, Nr. 10

In dieser Transkription eines Liedes von Clara Schumann zeigt sich der Bearbeiter Liszt von seiner besten Seite. Das unaufdringliche Arrangement konzentriert sich lediglich auf das Gleichgewicht zwischen Melodie und der Begleitung aus gebrochenen Akkorden, so dass die Musik ihre eigene Geschichte erzählen kann. Beim Erlernen dieses Stückes kann es hilfreich sein, die Melodietöne zunächst etwas lauter zu spielen, zumindest, bis *alle* Sechzehntel gleich lang und sicher gespielt werden können. Ein wichtiger Aspekt der Melodienotation und somit auch der Interpretation ist der Unterschied zwischen zwei punktierten Achteln (Takt 1) und einer Viertel, auf die eine Achtel folgt (Takt 2).

Vergessene Romanze in e-Moll, S 527, LW A299

Dies ist die vom Komponisten selbst gekürzte und vereinfachte Transkription eines Stückes, das ursprünglich ca. 89 Takte hatte. Sie enthält zwar das Wesentliche des Originals, verzichtet aber auf eine Kadenz und eine Passage mit aufeinanderfolgenden arpeggierten Figuren. Das Gleichgewicht zwischen Melodie und Begleitung in Takt 17 bestimmt das Gesamttempo des Stückes. Am besten wählt man anstelle eines langsameren Tempos ein bewegtes Tempo, da es verhindert, dass die Akkorde der linken Hand die Melodie übertönen.

Nils Franke

Teaching and Learning Commentary

Walzer in A major, S 208a , LW A2, No. 2
The earliest piece in this collection, here is music that lives off the contrast between *legato* and *staccato* melody notes.

Mariotte – Valse pour [? de] Marie in A flat major, S 212a, LW A82
Neither virtuosic, reflective, religious, or dramatic, this little waltz seems far removed from whatever perspective one might have of Liszt. Instead, it is testimony to Liszt's ability to charm, to be light-hearted and care-free. Taken from a letter he wrote to Marie d'Agoult, it is a short but beautifully balanced trifle, in the best sense of the word. The melodic line of the work is embedded in the first note of each group of triplets, as marked by the composer from bar 17 onwards. To develop a fluent performance speed as soon as possible, practise each group of triplets as crotchet chords before playing it as written.

Magyar in B flat minor/G minor, S 164e
Liszt was no stranger to re-cycling or revising ideas, re-focussing whole works even, sometimes over a period of many years. Though not intended for publication, this album leaf, based on three familiar tunes from later in his output, makes an excellent 'Hungarian Rhapsody in minia-ture'. The most demanding material is arguably in the central *piu animato*, not least because of the stretch required in the left hand. For the piece to work as a whole, make the final *rallentando* a clear arrival point, both dynamically and in terms of timing.

Albumblatt No. 1, in E major, S 164, LW A66
The opening of this piece may seem unexpected. The augmented chord that resolves onto the second beat of the subsequent bar really does need to lead *across* the bar-line. Imagine the B♯ to be subject to a gradual *crescendo*, almost like a woodwind note, to enable a better sense of connection to the following C♯.

Feuilles d'Album in A flat major, S 165, LW A104
This is a sparkling encore, a Lisztian take on the waltz idiom which was so popular at the time. The fingering provided may not seem very comfortable at first, but the melodic material from bar 13 onwards doesn't leave much room for alternative fingering solutions, suggesting that one has to learn to 'mould the fingers round the keys' by making a particular finger work over a period of time. The sugge-sted division of passages between both hands is entirely editorial, but also practical! It is governed by the idea that in the end it is the sound that matters, rather than how it is produced.

Albumblatt in Walzerform in A major, S 166, LW A83
Though musically straight-forward, this is a useful piece in the combining of octaves in the right hand and leaps in the left. For as long as the weaker beats in the left hand are subservient to the melodic line, the piece will play itself. Look out for a somewhat unexpected modulation to C sharp major in bars 14/15.

Ländler in A flat major, S 211, LW A95
In the opening eight bars Liszt embeds the melody of the right hand into a continuous flow of quavers. To help de-velop a better aural concept of the relationship between bass and treble, practise these bars omitting all non-melody notes in the right hand.

Klavierstück No. 2 in A flat major, S 189a, LW A116
The main challenge of the initial eight bars is the effective separation of melody and accompaniment in the right hand. The supporting quaver figuration of these bars returns as double notes in bars 9 and 10, a texture that sounds quite similar in spirit to some of the accompanying passage-work in one of Liszt's most successful lyric concert pieces, the *Bénédiction de dieu dans la solitude*. Much of the effect of the piece lies in the timing of melody lines, which, in terms of 19th century performance practice, may not always coincide with the bass notes on the first beat of every bar. If you do decide to (marginally) delay the first melody note in a bar, rather than play it together with its corresponding note in the left, use the effect sparingly and at only pivotal points of the melody line.

Notturno No. 2, in E major, 1st version, S 541a [192a]
This 21-bar miniature is a beautifully balanced ABA struc-ture. Only the central section, bars 9-12, deviate from an otherwise treble orientated sound world: here both soprano and tenor line need to be clearly audible. The right hand fingering in bar 9, based on Liszt's own, enables the first four quavers to be played in one hand position. Leaning to the right, the hand then glides to the next position.

La cloche sonne, S 238, LW A169
This is one of the most technically accessible of Liszt's works. Somewhat of an album leaf in length and spirit, the work's main musical challenge is to balance melody and accompaniment, the former switching between the left hand in the outer sections and the right hand in bars 13-25. In the absence of any performance indications in the Weimar autograph, dynamics and articulation marks are entirely editorial, and as such discretionary.

Klavierstück in F sharp major, S 193
This piece alludes to the recent past and near future of its day. Somewhat reminiscent of Chopin's Barcarolle Op. 60 in key, rolling left hand figuration and use of thirds in the melodic line, it looks forward to late romantic French and Russian music. The *quasi* cadenza in bars 22-24 generates the dynamic climax of the whole piece. Much of the musical unrest is derived from the tension between a descending chromatic harmony versus the rhythmic characterisation of a sequence of two quavers within a three quaver pattern. The thirds from bar 30 onwards are best learnt as a sequence of crotchet chords, involving whatever notes make up the thirds on each respective beat.

Kleine Klavierstücke, S 192, LW A233

These five works, written as individual miniatures over a period of fourteen years, cover the time in which the composer's style moved from the expressive lyricism of his major works to an increasingly introspective and harmonically experimental framework. The stylistic simplicity of the first two numbers still incorporates Lisztian features: the end of No. 2 (from bar 43 onwards) uses left hand figurations in which the fifth finger follows the first (bar 44); a technique Liszt used to spectacular effect, albeit in the right hand (consequently fingers 5 to 1), in the scale passages of his *Rhapsodie espagnole*. Nos. 3 and 4 are thinner in texture, and calmer in mood, but the fifth piece, *Sospiri*, is arguably the musically most innovative of the set. Though the arpeggiated left hand patterns, bars 38-57, do offer harmonic resolutions, the end of the piece does not - the resulting musical question mark being a direct manifestation of the future uncertainty that was to face tonal music, or so it seems in retrospection at least. The arpeggiated figures enable two different approaches to fingering, as indicated in the score. It might be beneficial to study both, not least because, based on the fingering used, the sound of this passage can vary noticeably.

Geheimes Flüstern hier und dort, S 569, LW A264b, No. 10

This transcription of one of Clara Schumann's songs shows Liszt the arranger at his most subtle. The understated adaptation concentrates only on the balance between the melody and the accompaniment figuration of broken chords, leaving the music's inbuilt narrative to tell its own story. In learning this work it may help to play the melody notes a little firmer at first, at least until *all* the semiquavers are even and securely in place. An important feature of the melodic writing, and thus of any performance, is the difference in timing between two dotted quavers (bar 1), and a crotchet followed by a quaver (bar 2).

Vergessene Romanze in E minor, S 527, LW A299

This is the composer's own shortened and simplified transcription of a piece initially running to some 89 bars. It presents the essence of the original but omits a cadenza and some arpeggiated, sequentially enhancing, passage-work. The balance between melody and accompaniment in bar 17 determines the overall tempo of the work. Choosing a moving, rather than slower tempo, works best, as it prevents a build-up of left hand harmony from overpowering the melody.

Nils Franke

Romantic Piano Anthology

**Original Works from the Romantic period
Selected and edited by Nils Franke**

- Both mainstream and lesser-known works from composers such as Chopin, Schumann, Gounod and Rimsky-Korsakov

- Graded pieces new to the graded framework presented in a progressive order

- Extensive commentary on each piece

- Composer biographies included

- CD recording of all the pieces played by Nils Franke

Volume 1 (Grades 1-2) ED 12912	**Volume 2** (Grades 3-4) ED 12913
Volume 3 (Grades 5-6) ED 12914	**Volume 4** (Grades 7-8) ED 12915

"This is a lovely book reflecting Schott's renowned high standards and interest in piano pedagogy."

Romantic Piano Anthology 2 - **Music Teacher Magazine**